FIND • DISCOVER • LEARN

T0002614

BIG
BOOK OF

Zodiac Signs

CLEVER
• Publishing •

This book belongs to:

_____

The 12 Signs of the Zodiac

ARIES

March 21 – April 19

You strive
to be the best.

Brave

You have
so much energy!

Strong

Confident

Your color is red.

Your gemstone is diamond.

Your flower is honeysuckle.

You might grow up to be...

a doctor

an inventor

an athlete

an engineer

No matter what you become, you'll have LOTS of loving friends!

TAURUS

April 20 – May 20

Creative

Strong

You like having
a steady routine.

Down-to-earth

You're warmhearted
and dependable.

Your color is pink.

Your flower is the poppy.

Your gemstone is emerald.

You might grow up to be...

a performer

a chef

an architect

a gardener

For a multitalented kid like you, the sky's the limit!

N 175

GEMINI
May 21 – June 20

Intelligent

Passionate

You're a social butterfly.

You're very curious.

Loyal

Your flower is lily of the valley.

Your color is teal!

Your gemstone is moonstone.

You might grow up to be...

a computer technician

a teacher

a musician

a dancer

With your skills and ambition, you're an unstoppable superstar!

CANCER

June 21 – July 22

Creative

Imaginative

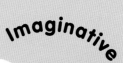

You're a
creative dreamer.

Curious

You are loving
and kind.

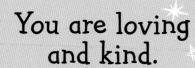

Your colors are blue and silver.

Your gemstone is ruby.

Your flower is the white rose.

You might grow up to be...

a baker

a nurse

a social worker

a designer

a therapist

You can become anything you desire!

LEO

July 23 – Aug 22

You are loyal.

Loving

Fearless

You're cheerful and fun.

Confident

Your colors are gold and orange.

Your flower is the sunflower.

Your gemstone is amber.

You might grow up to be...

a politician

a physicist

$E = mc^2$

a biologist

a movie star

No matter what you become, the spotlight will always shine on your sparkling personality!

VIRGO

August 23 – September 22

You want to know and understand everything!

Genuine

Motivated

Inquisitive

You're smart and love to learn.

Your gemstone is jade.

Your color is navy blue.

Your flower is the morning glory.

You might grow up to be...

a lawyer

a veterinarian

a conductor

a botanist

Your curiousity means you'll always uncover something new and exciting!

LIBRA

September 23 – October 23

Peacekeeper

You're fun to be around.

You're charming and easygoing.

You're a great communicator.

Musical

Generous

Your colors are blue and lavender.

Your flower is the rose.

Your gemstone is opal.

You might grow up to be...

a judge

an archaeologist

an animal activist

a reporter

With your sweet personality, you're always in harmony with your surroundings.

SCORPIO

October 24 – November 21

You're one cool friend.

Trustworthy

You're confident and give great advice.

Witty

Imaginative

Your color is dark red.

Your gemstone is topaz.

Your flower is the chrysanthemum.

You might grow up to be…

a translator

a therapist

a detective

a librarian

Everyone wants to be your friend!

SAGITTARIUS

November 22 – December 21

Generous

Optimistic

You're fun-loving
and friendly.

Dynamic

You love an
adventure.

Your flower is the daffodil.

Your color is purple.

Your gemstone is sapphire.

You might grow up to be...

a party planner

an astronaut

a photographer

With your free spirit, the world is yours to explore!

a race car driver

CAPRICORN

December 22 – January 19

Successful

Hilarious

You play hard and have a great sense of humor.

You're a natural leader.

Ambitious

Your flower is the carnation.

Your colors are green and brown.

Your gemstone is garnet.

You might grow up to be...

a mathematician

a health-care worker

a poet

an environmentalist

No matter where you're headed, you'll make it to the top!

AQUARIUS

January 20 – February 18

Beloved

You're one smart cookie.

Original

You're a free spirit who loves new things.

You're cheerful and friendly.

Your flower is the violet.

Your color is sky blue.

Your gemstone is jasper.

You might grow up to be…

a meteorologist

a computer coder

a sculptor

a professor

Your future is as bright as you are!

PISCES

February 19 – March 20

Builder

Graceful

You like to dream big!

You're a great problem solver.

Crafty

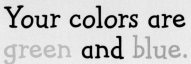

Your colors are green and blue.

Your
gemstone is
amethyst.

Your flower is
the water lily.

You might grow up to be…

an artist

a writer

a jeweler

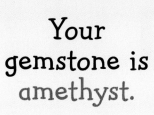

an actor

No matter
what you do,
you'll discover
all kinds of
things!

ARIES

MARCH 21–APRIL 19

TAURUS

APRIL 20–MAY 20

GEMINI

MAY 21–JUNE 20

CANCER

JUNE 21–JULY 22

LEO

JULY 23–AUGUST 22

VIRGO

AUGUST 23–SEPTEMBER 22